# Evelina Grava

# PSYCHOTHERAPY HANDBOOK

## Practical examples

# REFINED EVIL:

## Physical & visual manifestations of evil

*Second Edition*

# CONTENT

# HEALTH &
# PSYCHOLOGY

I will not be lying to the reader if I say that everything that is psychosomatic is linked to emotional discomfort. Emotional disturbances are reflected in physical health and in our history of illness. If we have "twisted" thoughts, we provoke our physical body into suffering pain and disease. Our physical body "twists" along with our emotions, and it loses balance. All that remains is to see the direction in which the imbalance moves.

According to psychosomatic theory, each organ relates to emotional experiences. There can, for instance, be different kinds of back pain, but essentially back pain tends to relate to a lack of inner stability. If you feel a sense of weight on your shoulders, you're suffering too much concern or difficulty. If you feel pain between your shoulder blades which causes you to bend over, that indicates that you yield too much and have too little in the way of durability. Headaches? "Too many contradictions I have to deal with!" Not all headaches are the same. If the pain is in your forehead, that may indicate that you are spitefully banging your head into the wall. If the pain is in your temples, that indicates that you suffer from perfectionism and a desire for recognition in the eyes of others. That means tensions that pulsate in your head and sometimes convulsively remind you of the fact that an individual's thoughts are artificial, that they lack naturalness and respect for themselves. High blood pressure, too, reveals our emotions and our needs. It shows that we are in a place that is just too narrow or small for us. The blood wishes to stream more rapidly, but they lack room in our veins. Our ambitions are not satisfied. Men aged between 40 and 50 are in the risk group for hypertension. That is a significant fact, because it indicates an age-related crisis. Excessively low blood pressure, in turn, is a sign of weariness.

Please let's remember that we can grow tired of ourselves. Lower immunity relates to different allergies. The body cannot oppose these problems, and the same happens with our emotions. Children suffer from paediatric diseases in childhood and form immunity which means that they will not suffer aggressive diseases in the future. The most common cause of illness in children is not the season of the year. It has to do with new social contacts instead. When a child goes to kindergarten, takes part in an interest group, or goes to school, that means that an emotionally complicated stage in life has begun. The world of small children is narrow – mom, dad, the children themselves. Then come new and unknown attitudes and situations. The small child may feel that the entire world is collapsing – he or she has no experience, and it is not at all easy to accumulate it very quickly. As children experience new situations, they discover new rules which they must place into their own lives. Time is needed if this is to be an unforced situation. The most optimal process of systematising the new information is to get sick for awhile. At this age, this is psychologically healthy self-protection to avoid damage to the psyche. Instead, children can thus mature a bit and prepare themselves for the next round of information that is coming. This is an age at which something new is happening every day. The teacher may be wearing a new dress. A chair may be somewhere other than where it used to be. Lunch arrives too quickly. These are all things which children have to consider very actively. Naps are meant specifically so that the child's brain can rest for a bit. Children refuse to take a nap when they're able to absorb a greater amount of information and when they have their own ideas about life. Perhaps you've noticed that children play differently with playmates of the same age group if they are at different locations – at home, out in the garden, at the playground, at the beach, at the kindergarten, etc. That's because some children form psychological comfort, and others do not.

What exactly does psychological comfort mean? In this case, it means that children are prepared to accept the emotional contacts for which they have been prepared so that they could grow up in a productive way. There are children who are not prepared to share their toys. If this upsets them negatively, that probably means that they have not yet learned to respect others. Such children won't want to meet their playmates a second time, because they know that there's no point in playing if the relationship is a bad one. Instead, there's a lot of crying, whinging, yelling and fighting.

Refined evil occurs when children are forced to understand things that are not in line with their internal level of learning about life. Everything happens eventually, but always at its own pace and in a logical sequence. The psyche is a very clear and harmonic mechanism. It expands and develops in accordance with specific laws related to nature and one's internal development. If parents force a child to understand something that is not yet naturally understandable, then the child's mental and physical health will suffer. If a small child starts to object to something that seems unnecessary, the response from parents will too often be moralising and an attempt to discredit the child. Sometimes this happens in the presence of other adults or children, and parents claim that this is a process of raising kids. Parents are very afraid of a situation in which others feel that their child has not been raised properly. That could be, but it does not apply to an example that we can consider here. Emotional readiness and child rearing are not one and the same thing.

Consider a four-year-old girl who is being visited by a two-year-old boy. The girl's room is neat and tidy. Everything was in perfect order. When she finished playing with toys, she always put them back where they belonged. The little boy, however, tried to grab every toy that he could see and consider it his own. He loudly announced that he was taking the toys home with him. The little girl tried to take her toys back. The boy responded by trying to bite her. Of course that hurt, and the girl started to cry. She cried not just because she felt pain, but because of the conflict itself. The parents of the two children responded. The little girl's mother worried that her child might be an egotist who does not know how to share with other children, while the boy's father was concerned that the boy might grow up to be a thief and a hooligan. It is false to think that events like this promote the likelihood that such things will really happen. The age difference between the two kids makes it clear that they had different levels of psychological maturity. A four-year-old cannot understand that a two-year-old is younger and acts differently for that reason. Neither could the little girl really understand the boy was not yet capable of thorough speech and that her toys were surely not going to be taken away. At her age, the little girl believed that such aggressive behaviour was in line with the truth. She could not know that aggression is based on a lack of internal self-confidence and a fear of a certain type of "castration" – ending up without any toys at all.

Lots of people say that they when they reach the age at which they are conscious about their lives, they feel various unpleasant physical dysfunctions which place them in front of the choice that lots of people experience – suffer pain or reach for the pain killer. Hardly anyone today makes do without medical treatment or medications. If there's to be an operation, anaesthesia will be mandatory. In the case of a headache, however, there are different options. If a physical ailment cannot be diagnosed, it is usually classified as a psychosomatic problem. Medics sometimes write down the words "problems with the vegetative nervous system," and when the patient reads that diagnosis, it can be hard to understand the link between problems with the nervous system on the one hand and bothersome kidney pain on the other.

So what is the linkage between nerves and kidneys? The patient can seek a second opinion, and the second doctor can either reaffirm the initial diagnosis or reject it. Either decision is possible. The kidney pain may not relate to psychosomatic problems, because there can be other causes for it. Sometimes people are just tended toward getting sick.

We know a lot about people today. We can inherit the genes of our parents, and we do. These are in close linkage with psychological processes. In this case, the kidney may be sending a "message from the dynasty." This is something common and unifying that has been inherited without the person realising it. Psychotherapists can discover this and make sure that the diagnosis is not passed down to future generations. Various areas of psychotherapy have had quite a few successful cases of this kind. Such results are described in the scientific literature, but also in fiction. There's a novel in which the heroine is threatened by a lethal disease which is identified and prevented with the help of a psychotherapist, thus stopping the flow of "generational messages."

We have already discussed the fact that each of us has different heredity. Some of us have deeply rooted teeth and bit teeth that don't nicely fit into a small jaw. The teeth may be coming from the father, while the jaw comes from the mother. The father has been generous with his teeth, but he has not sent along an appropriately large jaw. Perhaps in this case he wanted to be polite enough to allow his wife to contribute the jaw.

One can try to understand trends in mutual relations and heredity, but that is something that is close to soothsaying. The same is not true with psychosomatics, which has been studied and described scientifically. Psychosomatics start where objective medical conclusions end. There are chronic diseases, however, which grow worse because of long-lasting psychosomatic conditions.

# SELF-THERAPY AT HOME

Because our flesh and spirit are unified, we can sense that causes are based not on our bodies, but on our feelings and our perceptions. People can feel grouchy and dissatisfied for years on end. Women grump at their husbands and children. They only smile when the situation demands it, and they can hardly ever rid their faces of tension. The clothes that such women wear don't fit properly, their hairstyles are not what they want them to be. Life goes on, but such women have no internal spark.

The manifestations are similar for men. They can be just as grouchy as women can, and they tend to feel bad when they look in the mirror even if they are good looking. Men also want the internal spark. Our bodies have memories, just like our minds do. Our minds remember a poem that we learned at school, while our bodies remember habits, senses of comfort or discomfort, slimness, weight, cold and hot. Of course, that all has to do with our brains, but the information arrives in the brain via the body. If your body touches a small child and feels the warmth of the child, the brain creates recognition. Even modern automobiles are equipped with the body language of the driver – the computer recognises the driver and adjusts the seat appropriately.

I would like to continue the discussion about things that may be less thoroughly researched. The issue here is not that the brain sends signals to the body, but that the body also provides information to the brain. Why is that necessary? It's because there are things that cannot always be fully explained in scientific terms. This is gestalt.

If you have no bodily experience, then you cannot understand your desires and your needs. If you have not enjoyed the touch of a masseur, for instance, you probably will not seek another massage. If there are things that you have not enjoyed, then in bodily terms, you may very well not desire them at all. If you have never had enjoyable sex, then you can see sex as something that is simply capricious. The laziness of your body suggests that it lacks new experiences. Get busy – exercise, go swimming, go running. Move, in other words, and you will notice first of all that you will be unable to live without such movements in your life, and second that your intellectual potential will be higher. Exercise sends information to the brain. You engage in ever more complicated movements, and that expands your range of view. In anatomic terms, you do not always realise exactly what is happening and which of your muscle groups are involved in the process, so your job is to perform the exercise as precisely as possible so as to satisfy your need to move.

You move, and you feel good. You shouldn't just exercise your mind. Your body needs exercise, too. Exercise is particularly advisable for children, because that develops and matures them. The physical body is very wise. It is an outstanding computer, and you need to learn to listen to this mechanism. Think about creative ideas which relate to your body. Put a chair in front of yourself and sit down in front of it. Find out why your body is not happy and satisfied. You need to restore the dialogue between body and mind, because it has become too weak. Please don't mix this up with your brain and neurology. The mind is what philosophers describe in their theses.

One of the simplest methods for strengthening the emotional link between body and mind is one that can be used by anyone. Make sure that you won't be disturbed. Shut off the phone, close the door and, if you like, turn on some music. Take the same chair and yield before your moods. Every thought that comes to mind is there for a logical and systemic region. The words may seem unrelated and un related to one another, but there is logic in them – you just need to understand that. Don't worry if the words do not pour into your mind all by themselves, nor should you try to sop them if they become a torrent. The instructions have been delivered, and you already know that your body is in front of you now in a sense. Your job is to visualise it and see what is unusual, interesting or familiar therein.

Take a deep breath and don't be in any hurry. You're facing a mutually serious conversation. The goal is to return the spark to your physical body. You can ask yourself why you get sick, why you don't exercise, why your body isn't happy, and why it does not want to be close to another body.

The next important task is to wait for the answer. Change places. You sit in the other chair, and let your "body" take your chair. This little psychodrama can offer you the first motivation to become more interested in yourself. Of course, self-analysis is not an unambiguous process. It has its pluses and minuses. Still, you can use it to get at least some encouragement and some new ideas.

If you cannot accept this kind of contact with your own body or think that the process is too complicated or uninteresting, then sit down and write your body a letter. When it's ready, "send it" to yourself. When opening it, read it as if you had not written it and were looking at it for the very first time.

If you want the communications process to be bilateral and successful, write back to yourself. Read the letter several times, because it will tell you where your spark in life has gone and how you can recover it. Your quality of life depends on this. It can encourage you to focus more attention on yourself and deal with your problems. First and foremost, you can get an understanding of your body, which is where your emotions and feelings reside. Of course, you have to visit doctors, but you have to visit them as professionals who can answer specific questions. You cannot hope that they will provide you with the love of a father and a mother.

Writing such a letter will not resolve your problem, but it will prepare you to visit a professional doctor. The letter forms a reciprocal link, but its level of analysis is limited. The reader can engage in independent thinking and gain an idea of methodological approaches. The author's interpretation must not, however, be seen as a textbook case or as a universal session of therapy.

Here are a few lines from a letter that was written to a body. The author was a woman called Rigonda who agreed to have the text published just because she wanted to receive analysis and comments from a specialist.

Rigonda is 47 and has been married for 25 years. She and her husband have two children who no longer live at home. Rigonda is, generally speaking, satisfied with her private life and her work, but over the last two years she has suffered irritating gynaecological infections. They disappear only to return in the same place. Rigonda was worried enough to stop visiting the doctor who apparently could not help her to get better. She started to think about a different approach of helping herself. One summer afternoon, she conducted an individual experiment, asking her husband to help out. He wrote down the words that she spoke during her self-therapy. Rigonda dictated the letter, When she was done, her husband folded the letter, put it into an envelope, and gave it back to his wife so that she could read it by herself. Here's what the letter said:

"Hello, my body. I've been friends with you all my life. A few formalities do not hinder our relationship, but recently I've noticed that you've become independent and are doing things that I cannot understand. I guess you don't like something, because you are constantly yeasty and delivering liquid that smells terrible from my vagina. I have tried to take care of you, and doctors have helped me, but you have become too fussy and sensitive. If you want this special approach, then I want to know what exactly you need from me. I really want to find out, and I hope that we can work together. I'm the closest person to you. Rigonda."

Later the woman said that after she read her own letter, she didn't understand anything. It seemed to her that it was a sign of desperation to write a letter to her own body and hope that the questions would be answered. She read the letter again and again, but she found nothing new that would allow her to prepare to visit a different doctor. Rigonda decided to forget about the letter and seek other ways of improving her health. She put the letter in a desk drawer and forgot all about it.

Two years passed. Rigonda's health did not deteriorate, but it also did not improve. One day she remembered the letter and was interested enough to read it again. This time she decided to answer from the perspective of her body:

"Hi, Rigonda. It's interesting that you've remembered about me, because I think it has been two years since I got your letter. As you can see, I can only answer your question now. Please don't be offended, but I was offended by some of the words that you used – *yeasty* and *terrible smell*. I am not yeasty or stinky unless you make me so. You are not just the author of the first letter, you are also writing my answer. I cannot talk, so I hope that you will understand the main thought that I wanted to transfer to yourself. With respect, your body."

The next letter was written quickly, and the third one was no problem either. Here's the answer:

"Hello, my body. I feel tingly. I feel with every nerve that the letter came from a man. I'm fascinated by how specific your thoughts are and how much you feel self-respect, because you speak of yourself openly. You're certainly a man, and your letter hides deep offence which you really want to deal with in relation to a woman, to me. I felt that your writing style was even erotic. I could never have imagined that the text would excite me so much. I want to answer you not just in writing, but also physically. I feel the smell of your skin, I feel your muscles and your body. If only I could, I would ask you for sex as if I were asking you to dance. I can't wait for your answer."

The pen didn't even leave the paper. Rigonda immediately started to compose the reply:

"My darling. It turns out that I was impulsive, but you had depressed me. You used me, took advantage of me, regulated me, commented about me and criticised me. It started long ago. When I offered closeness to you, you always found reasons to avoid me, you always had excuses. You know better than I do that you can always find a reason and an excuse – weariness, a bad mood, jealousy, an uncomfortable bed. I have to say, however, that that was not always the case as we lived together. After we had our children, you drew away from me. I could no longer reach you. That was exactly when you distanced yourself from me, although I have always desired you and desire you now even more than then. You are the loveliest and most tempting woman in the world. I'm waiting for you. Your body."

The answer was written without rereading the letter. There was a dialogue now, and Rigonda was aware of it. She hurriedly wrote another answer, a more concrete one, but this time it was to her husband. She had no doubt that it was he who had written:

"My darling husband. I won't use any cute word for you now, because I feel you as a partner. I understand that now, and I feel so fantastic! I feel desired, and what you said confirmed it to me. My feelings allow me to believe that I am tempting you. At my age, that is an enormous revelation, because I was deeply, deeply convinced that I could no longer excite you. Please believe what I wrote just a few minutes ago. You're right – I'm yeasty because I have internal disharmony, and I have to think about why I was in such a hurry to write myself off... And as soon as I finished that last sentence, I remembered that mama taught me from childhood that eventually the relationship between a woman and a man grows boring and that the level of mutual interest naturally diminishes after children are born. She told me that a man will always try to find something more interesting. It is the nature of men to look for a "fresher" and tighter body, because women are always destined to lose their looks. Now I need to rest for awhile. I'll have some coffee, I'll think about this, and then I'll answer you some more. I wish you the very best. Your wife."

This time there was a longer pause. Rigonda knew that she wanted to continue the correspondence, but she no longer saw the point to the dialogue. She found that her problems had nothing to do with her husband. Of course, her husband was a unique intermediary between Rigonda and her mother. It was specifically when she was in contact with her "husband" that she realised what she was considering in her subconscious, and she knew where she could find the cause. Her mother didn't know that she had passed on a specific formula about the relationship between a husband and a wife to her daughter.

This situation was a model which shows how the sexual life of women must continue from generation to generation, because this particularly family was one in which there was a predisposition for cancer. Many of Rigonda's female relatives had undergone operations and other procedures.

When a woman faces Rigonda's situation, she most often starts to quarrel with her husband. This quarrel has nothing to do with what the husband has done, it is based on an attitude that the woman has inherited. She cannot demand from her husband that which he already provides and is prepared to continue to provide. Perhaps he will say the same thing again and again: "I am prepared to accept you, I want you, you excite me." And yet the woman may be unable to hear him. She may not recognise the symbols. She may continue to talk about the confirmations of attention which, in truth, she should be demonstrating toward her husband.

The first letter, let's remember, was written two years before the body was prepared to answer. What does that suggest? Apparently the woman subconsciously wanted to get rid of something important. She told herself that the letter writing was just silly. That can happen, and people cannot independently deal with such psychological opposition. The good news is that over the course of the two years when Rigonda was preparing herself in psychological terms, her body also took a break and did not move in either direction. That is an ideal situation for a transitional phase in life when the first step has been taken and the person needs to prepare for the next one.

The fact that Rigonda would reveal her relationship with her husband during the correspondence was clear from the very beginning, because she had asked him to take part in the process. Her husband showed his attitude toward his wife at that time, because he was not just responsive, but also tolerant toward what she wanted. Rigonda wanted him to help her with part of the job, but she also wanted to maintain intimacy. Sex may be fully in line with this description. When they were close, the partners opened up to one another, but they preserved their individuality. What's more, sexual closeness is not the only sign of intimacy. Emotions and feelings are important, too. In this case, the husband demonstrated this to his wife. He was aware of the content of the letter, but he felt that opening the envelope and reading the letter was a personal process for his wife. It's not acceptable to open someone else's mail even if you've had a sexual relationship with that other person.

The reader may naturally be interested in knowing what happened next. First of all, we can look at how the woman's attitude toward her husband developed. Second, we can ask whether her health changed. Third, we may be interested in what was happening with the gender message that her mother had transferred to her. Refined evil walked right past this woman's door, it has to be said. There were lots of reasons to provoke it, too. The woman could start open conflicts against her husband. The husband wouldn't understand her behaviour and would perhaps flee. There are all kinds of considerations as to whether one should or should not become involved in this problem. The husband could react with apathy or the complaints that were discussed before. These are disputes which cause families to fall apart, because the true reason for the conflict is unknown, and that means that the discussion is about everything other than the true cause of the difficulties. That is only logical. The roots of a plant are usually not aboveground. They are covered with soil. People, similarly, make decisions on the basis of external expressions.

The views and instructions which a woman receives from her parents affect her health and the happiness of her family. The same is true with predictions that parents have made about different situations. The main thing here is that the woman has heard these words and has subconsciously held on to them. There are at least two different ways in which the messages of our parents can reach us. Parents can purposefully give us information so as to teach us something, protect us, keep us from doing things, etc. It is also possible, however, that parents can say things which children must interpret on the basis of what they know at that time. How much can a child know about the relationship between an adult woman and an adult man? They know something, of course, but surely not as much as their parents do.

# THE TRUTH ABOUT SEX AND FEELINGS

What should parents do, in that case, to avoid transferring things to the next generation? Parents have to share that experience. That is necessary, but the effort must be to make sure that knowledge is presented not as a claim, but instead as a discussion about the unique experience of the specific person. It is important to understand that parents must not seem absolutism. They must instead speak to a small part of that which happens in the world between women and men. This is a far gentler approach, and it does not sound dangerous in that the child then has every opportunity to choose a different model for his or her relationships. Frustrating positions can be changed this way.

Rigonda had several possibilities in her life. She could have joined with her mother in opposition to her husband. The coalition then would have had this slogan: "A woman who has given birth is never sexually attractive to a man." Both women would have unconsciously projected this idea. The husband would not have had problems in terms of having sex with his wife. The woman is the one whose perception changes after she has her children.

It is always possible to find yes-men in life. Some women don't think for themselves, choosing instead to yield before public pressure. The experience of parents, friends, acquaintances and neighbours, the media, the cinema, and so on. The thing is that the focus of attitudes can differ. One woman will be unhealthily worried about her weight and her body proportions, another will be upset about her age or the approach of menopause, and so on. We can always find problems, and if we use them as a shield, then we can no longer have any objective thoughts. Sometimes it really is a sad thing that women treat themselves as objects, without sufficient self-respect. What is unique is that such sexually unsatisfied women merge into interest groups. They hope to improve and maintain their knowledge and skills via a hobby which allows them to divert their sexual energy.

Rigonda, too, could have become an activist in some women's club which ensures a hidden and subconscious war against men. Perhaps she would not have discovered that which she learned through the letters if she had not had her health issues. In such cases, women should not sit around and wait to get sick. They should instead make sure that they don't get sick. It is easier than easy to check out your need to revisit your psycho-emotional difficulties or complications. You need only to spend a bit of time in the past to make an attempt at an intellectual explanation of the present, of your emotional and physiological tensions, and your ability to take an adult look at your childhood events and the role which your parents played therein. Your ancestors consciously and subconsciously wrote a letter and sent it to you. When you open and read it, you can learn about your own body. It's an archive. It represents a real opportunity to receive answers to your questions, and that, in turn, allows you to learn about and predict the future. It is said that the apple does not fall far from the tree. You can find out for yourself whether that's true in your life. There are probably children who "fall" a bit too far. They become thieves and scoundrels, even though that may be a manifestation of revenge against something unknown, unexpressed and unhealed.

It is easy to understand what you need. As soon as you feel dissatisfied with yourself or your environment, you seek help. That is far more responsible and productive than to cause sickness and suffering in your children or to break up your marriage, thus making your children partial orphans even though both of their parents are alive. The absence of both parents has a serious effect on the child's psychological world and perceptions about life. Don't think that children don't suffer. They feel pain even if they don't show it. Sometimes they take over the role of parents in relation to their own father and mother.

For this reason, if the author of this letter manages to take the next step in the right direction, she has every chance of becoming healthy, as well as sexually and emotionally satisfied with herself and her husband until old age. Adult children will not have to be shocked about the fact that their parents are getting divorced, as opposed to living happily together. The attention of the grandchildren will not have to be divided into two, and the younger generations will not be given the unfavourable message that when people get to middle age, they have to get divorced. Why should they have to? Not everyone will be prepared to admit to themselves and to others that misunderstandings could be resolved in a way that is different from the idea of "So you don't like something? OK, let's get divorced!"

Of course, as we look at what the author of the letter did after such a long pause, it is interesting and even important to learn at least a bit about the stages of her attempt to deal with the problem and the results of the process. The fifth letter can be characterised as a discovery after which there must be a long period of contemplation. Gestalt theory includes this thought: "Human reactions are absolutely true and adequate in a specific situation or environment." If you need additional time for further consideration, then take that time, but please don't forget that there will be an opposing force. We have the experience of what happened after the first letter – two years passed. As I mentioned already, the conclusion can be very different. Of course, we want there to be a positive result, but none of us can ever be certain of that.

German research into the effectiveness of psychotherapy is worth some consideration here, because, as it turns out, the greatest role in a successful psychotherapeutic session is played by the client, not by the psychotherapist's qualifications and experience. People can achieve a great deal on their own. There is no reason to question the statistics, because responsibility for the results of the study has been taken by the Centre for Psychotherapeutic Research in Stuttgart. My aim here is not to try to ignore the matter of professional responsibility, although it is true that we cannot exclude the possibility that a patient might lose his or her mind and then the psychotherapist or psychoanalyst analyses the risk, diagnosis and overall situation incorrectly, fails to show any interest in the patient, and hides behind the mystical smokescreen of ethics and confidentiality. There are cases in which we cannot ignore a lack of talent, a shortage of self-therapy, or weaknesses in terms of mental health, and yet the overall thought here is this: Don't give up if you fail at first. Continue to seek explanations despite your negative experience.

No professional will ever claim that unpleasant emotions, disappointment in the psychotherapeutic process or unhappiness with the psychotherapist is automatically a negative thing. All of the objects in a system can work together even if they are different and diverse. There is responsibility here, and it must certainly be undertaken by the patient, client, consultant and professional. If blind people ask blind people to teach them to see, if deaf people ask deaf people to teach them to hear, and if crippled people ask crippled people to teach them to dance, then we can foresee the result quite precisely. This would be a waste of time, money and hope. Frustration would become stronger, and that would nurture refined evil. It would be naive to think that you can receive something from someone which the other person does not even have. It would mean thinking that someone who is just like you is actually better than you. The Bible says that it is a sin to worship false idols. A person with no arm cannot grow a new one, and if someone promises the impossible, then that is a hiding of the truth; it is simply a lie.

No psychotherapist can ever promise that after a certain number of sessions, the client will lose weight, get rid of phobias, find a life partner, learn to make a living, and so on. The abilities of the analyst and psychotherapist are limited by the potential of the client or the patient. A paediatrician, for instance, can promise to treat a child's cough if he is able to do so. The illness can be controlled and influenced, but if there are exaggerated promises, the risk is that it will take longer for the child to get better. There can be unexpected side-effects, a new virus, a psychosomatic issue, and so on. All of that can wreck the great promise that was made at first.

We all have our own recipes and experiences in terms of being a provider or receiver of services. Greater respect, trust and results can be achieved if both parties are involved in the process and are flexible in their attempt to achieve the desired success. Let's look at nature again. You can plant two identical seeds in the same soil, but get very different results. One plant may not take root even though you did your very best to promote its growth. I've heard a guru in psychology saying that the human psyche is still linked to a "black box" which means that the results cannot always be forecast. Just think about the resources and influence which you have when it comes to yourself. These are psychological and physiological processes in the first place and spiritual and philosophical ones in the second place. If we want to, we can change our attitudes and values without any intervention from the sidelines. Rigonda made the choice. She decided to approach her husband and find out whether the things that she had imagined were real. In other words, she wanted to know whether he felt that she had become cool toward him in sexual terms, and sure enough, that is what she found out.

The woman had quietly been expecting just that claim, because that would affirm the purpose of the letters that she wrote. She could then prepare a further plan of action. And yet Rigonda also wanted to make sure that her husband really wanted to be closer to her. She asked nothing more. Instead she recalled pleasant events, situations and episodes in which a man's erotic attitude toward a woman could find expression. Would she reject such advances if there was no experimental methodology in the process and if the attitudes and level of attention were not correct? She found out that the attitude was sufficient. The husband told her that her body turns him on, but then she told him that at her age, no woman could excite a normal man. "You are beautiful. You have beautiful eyes and a beautiful body," he says. "Take a look at this part of me – look at the consequences of childbirth," she snaps back. Yes, there have been caresses and touches with respect to which the husband wanted an appropriate reaction. There were moments of fine attention – a vial of perfume on the pillow and airline tickets underneath it. The woman's memories were endless, and they filled her consciousness. And then, suddenly, she realised something: "I am more valuable than I had imagined!"

The next thing that Rigonda decided to do was to find out in person what she had sensed while alone. She contacted her mother and had a serious discussion about her mother's sex life with her father, as well as about her grandmother.

She learned that grandma had never talked about sex with her daughter. For one thing, back then women didn't really know how to talk about such matters. Second, Rigonda's mother was raised in a situation where she dared not broach the subject herself. That's why the mother and grandmother limited the discussion to a few opaque phrases which made it clear that there would be no discussion of men.

As far as Rigonda's mother could remember, her mother was always unkind toward her husband. He played the accordion, was a home builder, liked everyone, had beautiful curly hair, and remained slim until the end of his life. Upon hearing this, Rigonda imagined a rude grandma and a nice grandpa and started to wonder whether the problem had not been jealousy on the part of the grandmother. She thought about the fact that this was an old relationship – one that she was considering at a time when she herself was preparing to be a grandmother: "It's like I've found an old family heirloom, and I'm cleaning it up and fixing it. It's hard to understand. It's something that's wrinkled and dirty, it's lost colour and form." Rigonda did not know whether her grandmother had any real reason to be jealous, but she could be sure that in her relationship with her husband, grandma had devalued herself and that grandpa certainly was not pleased at having such an angry wife. Rigonda understood that during the past two years, she had moved quite far in improving herself and in realising things that she had not realised before. She was thankful for this "home method" and concluded the "conversation" with her body, thinking that eventually she would return to it, but at a much higher level of quality.

These types of self-therapy methods can be very effective, but there are two things that you need to bear in mind here. First of all, if you break a leg, you will be able to treat the injury yourself only up to a certain extent. In truth, the only thing that you can do yourself is ensure first aid to make sure that the injury is not made more severe. The other thing is that you may put too much faith in your self-therapy methods, believing that you can handle everything on your own and, thus, sinking into inappropriate self-love. Other authors, too, have expressed similar cautions about self-therapy, but the fact is that if you have at least a bit of hope about reducing the level of your psychological discomfort, then give it a shot.

# PSYCHOLOGICAL
# CAUSES OF ILLNESS

Now that we've learned about the link between family messages and illness, we can ask what other reasons there might be for the sickness. A doctor probably won't ever ask you why you've become sick right at this time and not some other, but if the question is posed, patients tend to speak to different circumstances, but not the events of their own lives. I wasn't dressed warmly enough. I was standing in a draft. I didn't sleep enough. I didn't take my vitamins. Those are the conditions of everyday life, and it is quite possible that the individual has faced those kinds of situations lots of times without getting sick at all.

We must, therefore, take a more complex look at situations in which someone's health deteriorates. Have you thought about the fact that an unclear situation at work can cause illness in your body? The inability to get out of a tense conflict in psychological terms will affect your body. All that is needed is for the situation to change toward the better, and you will immediately feel fine. Have you ever noticed that sometimes getting better is just as mysterious a process as getting sick in the first place?

I remember someone telling me that for decades he had suffered from migraines and had tried all kinds of treatments without success. He said that nothing helped until one day the pain disappeared and never came back. He decided that this was because of a specific person toward whose ambitions the patient had devoted too much attention. Once he realised this, his health improved. This might be the conclusion here: Sickness cannot break into your body if you have not created an opportunity for it to do so. Of course, we can never completely protect ourselves against illness, but we can make our lives easier by understanding psychosomatic processes and the causes of an unacceptable physical condition in a broader context.

You cannot escape death, but you can try to make it easier, a wise person has said. What does that mean? Well, if you know that you're not supposed to eat sweets, then don't. Think about what sugar is compensating for in your body in psychological terms? If your hand reaches for a drink so often that the process becomes uncontrolled, then raise the alarm, look for the causes, and understand that the consequences of your behaviour are completely unpredictable. Think about this particularly if you have family members who face the same problem. It will be painful, but it is a necessary observation.

Do try to change your attitude, your way of thinking and your perceptions about yourself and your life. Stop cultivating evil inside yourself. Treating yourself unkindly is terribly evil. In some religions, you would be utterly denounced, you would face public punishment and a lot of suffering. Of course, you cannot punish anyone more severely than you punish yourself. If you're not happy with your body, your health and your appearance, that is a very difficult situation for you, as it would be for anyone else. You don't even want to get out of bed. You can never set yourself free. Your life is dull, routine and boring.

Lots of books describe psychosomatics, and that is not something that we can deny. We should read those books and keep this fact in mind. I don't want to repeat myself, but the fact is that the fish rots from the head. It is also a fact that those who are around us will always see our true emotional condition. That is not something that we can hide.

# CHARACTER & EMOTIONAL STATE

Now let's turn to the most visible part of you, the part that you cannot hide from others, and the part that you see immediately when you look into a mirror. I'm talking about your physical appearance.

Now, don't think that an elegant lady and gentleman who have fine and well-dressed children and live in a fine and orderly environment exist completely without evil, while a homeless person, a street musician or the beggar on the street corner is much more evil and unhappy than the elegant people are. No, they are simply more destructive, but their internal conflicts may well be one and the same.

We have all encountered our own evil and that of others, and we have managed to deal with it to a greater or lesser extent. We can learn a lot about ourselves by seeing what we do in various situations and how we react to existing or new circumstances. Just as there is an aftertaste to food, we have emotions every time that we communicate with a known or unknown person. Those emotions can be very pleasant, unpleasant or neutral. The stronger the after-emotions of a conversation are, the more powerfully, importantly and destructively we grow tense or, on the contrary, gain greater emotional comfort that can lift us up or, to a certain extent, destroy us. If the contact has been satisfactory, we feel positive about it, while if the communications have been unsatisfactory, afterwards we feel rather upset and nervous. We experience an inner storm, and we become more offended and more utilised by our emotions. We seem to be concerned about this emotional situation and understand how destructive it, because subconsciously we know that such emotions are repeated again and again, and so something that we are doing is just completely wrong.

How, then, are our emotional experiences broadcast in our visual appearance? Let's start with overall appearance. Imagine in your head what a mature man and a mature woman look like. There can be all kinds of psychological interpretations, of course, but come up with a template. That is because there are stereotypes and desires in society which are precisely reproduced by brand names in the fashion industry.

Men cannot wear what boys wear, and women cannot wear what girls wear. Of course, you may question that statement, because after all, why shouldn't you put on something that makes you appear youthful? The point is that few people would agree that a physically mature individual who is dressed like a teenager looks younger or better than is actually the case. Let's not, however, talk about what is "permitted" or "not permitted." The important thing here is what we express about ourselves via our apparel and our behaviour. These are not just external elements, they are the skin of our soul, and so I wouldn't agree that our outer appearance is unimportant and that only that which is inside us and has nothing to do with the outer world really counts. A person who is loved will look like someone who is loved. Sadness chews us up.

You can try to look good, but your appearance will betray your emotions. Sometimes, when we yield before refined evil, it is possible that we can hide under the outer shell, but we don't achieve what we want to achieve in society, because people perceive us in the way that we present ourselves – phallic or castrated. Clothes tell everyone that there is something too much or too little, that something has been added or taken away. You can think about the clothes of phallic women and men and those of castrated women and men.

An elderly lady once told me that once she had passed through menopause and no longer was menstruating, she felt like a proper human being for the first time, because her mother had never allowed her to feel like a woman. That was understandable, because her mother was raising her family herself, and how could the woman have refused to help in raising her younger brothers? No matter what this woman has in her closet, she is not going to be able to put together a womanly appearance. She will lack eroticism. She will have to polish up her gender so that there are no differences of opinion or undesirable departures from the task assigned by her parents. The woman never did get married, though she had two daughters out of wedlock. Throughout her sexually active life she was tormented by powerful headaches and stomach spasms before and during her menstrual cycle. In other words, she was helpless, useless and unneeded by anyone for about 10 days each month.

In operas, the costumes of the characters are meant to transfer information to the audience about the era, the nature of the individual, his or her social origins, and even the thoughts, values and attitudes of the character. Life, however, is not theatre. It is more serious and more painful. You can try to reduce your own pain without psychotherapy by creating a stage image of yourself. We are the stars of our own lives, and the same laws of perception apply to us as to actors who are in a play. Our clothes can attract others, make us interesting, encourage us, or, alternatively, turn people away, disappoint or maybe entertain them. It can push others away in emotional terms. If we do not understand that, then our children may end up not comprehending it either.

The aforementioned lady's mother was a wonderful woman who did not want her child to suffer so immense a burden. Their lives were intolerable. There was no chance to think about psychology, because a war was raging outside. She had no husband, and apart from her teenage daughter, she had no one to help. There was no reason for gender differences, no reason for joy. Hard work was of value. The adult daughters of my client now resemble their mother. That is a tragedy, because there was no objective reason for that to happen. The client's two brothers grew up, because their mother and their sister helped them to do so. The boys grew up into men who are unable to present a physical appearance that would testify to their being respectable men. They don't emphasise their masculine appearance, they are shy, they are unaware of the role of identity. They feel like people without gender and think that their main value in life is the ability to be human beings. Exactly the same happened to the lady's daughters one generation on.

# PROHIBITIONS & PROVOCATIONS

Parents can express things with their clothing that they cannot explain in words. By using proportionally turned-around experience, they can move from visual symbols to verbal explanations. That is commendable. External transformations conjure up different emotions. The main thing is to communicate and explain the fact that as soon as the war is over or an adult appears, the girl will not have to suffer to the point where she has to sacrifice her own identity. The ban has already been heard. If the person to whom the ban applies does not have enough strength, then the person or entity that has issued the ban – the adult, the cultural environment, the politics – must purposefully lift it. Otherwise the person who has received the ban can feel guilty if he or she wants to return to the unrepeatable magic of gender. The sense of heaviness can be so powerful that the person doesn't even try to regain his or her identity. This is a matter of incommensurability.

Here's another example. A four-year-old girl had thin hair. The hairdresser recommended a boyish hairdo so that the hair would look healthier, thicker and more precisely cut. That is what happened. The girl's inexpressive curls were gone, and soon she had hair that was normal in volume and length. After the process ended, the little girl asked: "Am I a little boy now?" Everyone heard her. Luckily, the girl's mother had intuition and good psychological knowledge. Today the girl is an adult woman who is happy about her feminine identity. She doesn't remember the incident at the hairdresser's shop, but others have told her about it. Her mother told her about gender differences, about the way in which the roots of hair can be strengthened and about the traditions and therapies which relate to this. As soon as they left the hairdresser's shop, the mother bought her daughter a beautiful red hat with flowery decorations of the type that no boy would ever wear. That closed the topic forever – the girl always saw femininity as an inviolable component of her life even if short hair once again came into fashion. Haircuts and clothing do not always depict delicate conditions of identity and attitudes. Sometimes it's just a matter of fashion and taste.

When do we first start to think about our clothing? Well, each to his or her own, but it's around the age of five that a child can clearly decide to wear the green and not the red jacket. Parents can receive this information in different ways. They can continue to insist on the red jacket, or they can accept the child's choice. This may seem like a petty thing – who cares what the child wears at kindergarten? And yet it is fundamentally important for children to make such choices, because the issue of the jacket can help to shape their ideas about themselves. They're thinking for the first time how they appear in the context of others who are there. At kindergarten, there are both peers and adults – people of different ages and of both genders, and here is the start of new relationships. What's more, the surrounding society offers children information not only about their knowledge, but also their appearance.

If children do not learn about the nuances of difference early on, then it will be more difficult for them to understand requirements about clothing when they get older. They may go to the opera in a gym suit or wear a swimsuit to a celebration at a castle. Psychological capacities are influenced by emotions. A harmonic person will always dress appropriately. Child-rearing is acceptable to those who can, in psycho-emotional terms, regulate their destructiveness after frustration. For instance, such people shake the hand of a person with whom they had a disagreement the previous way. They know to wear a proper dress and hat when going to a funeral. They don't get drunk to the point where they mess up someone else's event.

It seems that these days, such inappropriateness is often seen as a misunderstood expression of freedom. This is not, however, something which speaks to emotional comfort. We are instead talking about a lack of knowledge and an ability to understand the psychological tensions in one's existence. If we feel comfortable with our emotions, then they will not appear externally in a peculiar way. If, however, we do not have this internal capability, internal alarm can be seen externally, too.

I trust that the reader will agree that apparel is not really a matter of financing, because the issue is not the cost or quality of items of clothing. Instead, the question has to do with attitudes and expression of same. This is one of the most primitive manifestations of refined evil, because it could be changed immediately if only people were prepared to look inside themselves without the negative baggage of the past. That usually cannot be done quickly or without a positive impulse which is important enough to overcome the previous frustration. This can refer to falling in love, strengthening one's self-respect, discovery of one's abilities and capabilities, very good news, an inheritance, travel, pregnancy, a new job, career growth, renovation of one's home, or moving house altogether.

Sometimes disaster brings liberation. If one's father dies, for instance, it may mean that the child finally feels liberated from his influence. Knowing that the person is no longer alive means that controlled and frustrated people can feel a sense of emotional and internal freedom. I am sometimes surprised at how often I hear my patients talking about their sense of guilt or regret about the positive emotions, joy about life and interest as a psychological capacity which they feel when one of their parents are no longer as young as they once were and can no longer influence the patients on an everyday basis.

Such thoughts are tormenting. Even if they mean that it is easier to understand oneself, it is necessary really to understand the painful and deep consequences of the influence. I once knew a middle-aged woman who for the first time allowed herself to put on some earrings and some bright red lipstick only after her mother had died. There was a man who started to wear jeans and sports shirts, bright neckties and expensive shoes everywhere, not just in the presence of his wife. This is by no means easy in psycho-emotional terms. It can be tormenting, because discovering truth and understanding before someone dies is not possible because of these complicated experiences – unless one happens to find the special help of a psychotherapist, a clergyperson or any other trusted person.

It is not easy to interpret such situations in general terms. There can always be hard-hearted objectivity. For instance, children can be happy about something, but their fathers may not like the laughter. As soon as the child is glad about something, the father shuts down the happiness, and that is painful. Children are afraid to object, not just because of the psychological rolls which children and their parents play, but also, for instance, because talking back to one's father means the breakdown of a sacral emotion – even if the child does not yet know the semantic meaning of this concept. Intimacy is a special emotion, and the loss of intimacy is similar to castration. What does "intimacy" mean in this situation? There is a special emotional link between children and their parents, and because this link is tremendously personal, it will be different than relations with other people. This intimacy is preserved even if the parents are away from the house on a 24/7 basis. Growing up is an emotional collapse between two people who are close. It is a loss which one really wants to postpone because of the fear that the idea causes. It's better to remain the child of one's father than it is to be an autonomous person who happens to have a father. It is psychologically complicated to accept relations between two individual objects. It is more comfortable to desire for emotional links. Separation hints that one person can make do without the over. That is a truly difficult conclusion if the child is worried about possibly offending the father or being different than the father. How can this be expressed? A different temperament, nature, desires, behaviour, values, attitudes and physical appearance.

Still, children do not want to tug the tiger by the tail, because they hate that animal as much as they love it.

Children and adults remember similar emotions from their childhood. There can be many objective reasons – poverty, depression in the family, a sad and angry family, etc. Many people find it hard to be naturally happy, because no seed is planted under such tough circumstances. This is the basis for one's perception in life. A psychologically stable person can ensure self-regulation so as to avoid the excesses that are absolute positivism and absolute negativism. Being happy just for the sake of being happy is the same as being sad just for the sake of being sad. The thought is very precise. In order to avoid a situation in which they are simply waiting for someone to die, people choose to flee. They run away from those who place a psychologically negative burden on their shoulders – a burden which seems all but unbearable. There are girls and boys who, when going to a dance, bring along hidden clothes and dress in the lavatory, changing clothes again once again before going home so as not to hurt mama. I heard a girl saying that once: "Mama has a difficult life, I don't want to hurt her by looking careless."

When it comes to the story about the jacket, children are interested in how parents will react to their announcement, because they feel that their desires and needs must be respected. The thoughts of parents about this are unimportant. Of far greater importance is what children expect from them – responsibility, acceptance, a positive reaction, understanding. If that is not the case, then children will doubt whether their choices and desires are correct, and that will be true not only on the specific date, but also in the future. When children grow up they want to leave a good impression on others. If they fail to do so, the desire can become dull to the point where people become apathetic as to how they look and, accordingly, how they feel.

People with self-respect show via their appearance that they are able to respect the presence of others. In that case we would no longer face a situation in which high-standing people allow themselves to wear gym shoes along with a tuxedo to a New Year's celebration. These are rules which are also ignored in the private arena. In a bedroom, a man or a woman can afford to get undressed and show underwear that hasn't been changed for a week, thus creating disgust in the spouse. No matter how wise or ideal in nature such people might seem, they will be uninteresting and stinky to a person who is healthy. This degradation occurs gradually. Over the course of time, the person in question won't even be bother by or interested in the process. Psycho-emotional feelings can become dull just like skills and talents can do.

I will repeat myself here, but the ability to differentiate among things must be trained. Small children can point to the different colours of two jackets and want confirmation as to whether or not they are on the right road. Children don't care about nuance or self-fulfilment. People who are always exactly the same, whether they are outdoors or at church, cannot emotionally link circumstances of various events. You don't wear everyday work clothes to a worship service on a holiday, after all. Children develop, and they see that it is not the case that everyone does what their parents do. This has nothing to do with love, nature, manifestation of love or education unless parents turn innovations into farces, disobedience and spite. It is quite possible that children want to save their best jacket for a holiday. These are nuances which put together the skeleton of one's attitude toward oneself and the world.

One reason why people get divorced is that sometimes they don't observe the principle of appearance which is in line with one's environment. They have different ideas about what the husband and wife must look like, and that is true even if they do not go into the matter in any depth. What appears is true attitudes and complaints which annoy the other and even cause disgust. This can include an unpleasant smell or haircut, facial appearances, manners, clothing and attitudes toward oneself. This is something which touches upon egoism. Looking at the other, one can ask oneself: "Is that what kind of person I am, too?" Even if the other person is the same, it is easier to try to change, abandon or criticise the other person than it is to try to get both of them to change together. Refined evil is an effort to bring the other person back and to decide to tolerate the situation just a bit longer. A wife leaves her husband, a husband leaves his wife, or they continue to live together in a hostile way without knowing why. The point is that sometimes a bit of energy has to be invested to "stretch upward." When couples don't understand their own laziness, they don't do anything but bang on about different nature, views and sexual approaches – something that is far, far from the truth. Sometimes one is amazed at how similar are two married people who ignore the similarity and simply get divorced. It is understandable that people don't look deeply into themselves if, in childhood, they had quarrels with their parents about jackets, but not about their demands, their views, and their qualitative changes in attitudes. If the whole process is based on visual facts, without the participants understanding why they are doing what they are doing, then they end up criticising other people's behaviour, choices, taste and style. Culture has a psychological effect on human behaviour. Objects create an emotional response. The sense of well-being can be strengthened or eliminated by a comfortable or uncomfortable chair, the wearing of different textiles, lighting or the arrangement of furniture in a room. The visual impression of a person or of flora and fauna will make emotions brighter. Behaviour and internal requirements about specific attitudes depend on this.

# CHARACTER AS AN OBSTACLE TO RELATIONSHIPS

For instance, what should a city's chief artist be thinking about? The issue is whether architecture is in line with the specific context of the surrounding environment. No matter how "free" or "comfortable" an architect may want to be, the fact is that these are requirements which cannot be ignored. An ugly apartment building cannot be erected among buildings of cultural and historical importance. Those who want to do so have to accept that the law does not allow them to do so. But what about those of us who wear inappropriate clothing? That is more of an individual question – I wear what I want to wear, and just try to tell me otherwise! It turns out that there are sanctions against us if we know too little about ourselves. These are not legal sanctions, of course, but they are psychological ones. People can decide that we appear inadequate and all wrong in terms of composition.

Sometimes it's hard to tell who's the boss and who's the subordinate – the mother or daughter, the patient or doctor, the student or professor. An inappropriate external appearance will create the relevant attitude and response from others. Perhaps you've heard someone say that another person did not behave properly. Perhaps you saw someone at a party who you thought was a waiter but was not. This is a situation that has been addressed in movies, jokes and novels. There are two choices here. You can use a stereotype to mislead people consciously or not, or you can choose a form of behaviour which is in line with the stereotype. When people are comfortable with their image, they have identified themselves and are happy. Others have no doubt about this.

Why? Because such people differ in the sense that in psychological terms, they perform their roles very well.

It is valuable to analyse every incident individually, because a person's external appearance cannot be adjusted if the encouragement does not come from that person specifically. Improvements are not possible without emotional motivation and psychological readiness. People can sink into self-satisfaction which means that they cannot be taught. They don't accept advice, they consider themselves to be stable and mature people who need no improvements. This attitude is strengthened by experience that has put the brakes on development. For instance, people can be disappointed in a method, their investment may not lead to the returns that they desire, they can be short-sighted, they can lack will and courage, and they can fail to think in global terms and come to the necessary conclusions. It is valuable to think about failures, find their causes, and create a system in which one can learn about new viewpoints, receive a reciprocal link and responses, watch those who have something to say, and define new missions. If, for instance, someone has had a bad experience on a trip and, therefore, does not want to go anywhere else, that does not mean that the person has to stop learning about the world. Instead, there must be a search for new opportunities to gain impressions.

One method in revealing one's problems is to engage in social training and group psychotherapy, because this creates a microcosm. Here's an example. There was a man who complained that he always left a bad first impression on women. He could ring a woman who interested him and arrange for a date, but as soon as they came face-to-face, the woman usually ran away. When he explained this problem to a group, one of the women who were presented pointed out that the man had no teeth. It had never occurred to the guy that his external appearance was the problem. No one had ever pointed to it, either. People don't always see themselves. They get accustomed to their own smell and are unaware of the fact that others may dislike it. It is also true that not everyone wants to force his or her viewpoint on another, interrupt other people, etc.

Of course, that doesn't happen to everyone when interest in self-improvement appears during a person's life. There are lots of people who will never face a similar situation, because they don't give a damn as to why it is difficult for others to get along with them. There will, however, always be scholarly interest in why this happens. It is because the individual has been of no importance or, alternatively, extremely important to his or her parents. In both cases, there was no criticism, instruction or influence, and that is where narcissism – that deep yearning to love oneself – takes root. If you're ideal, you don't need any advisors. If others want to draw close to you, then let them try. They need to accept you as a grown up child just the way that you are. If they don't like your appearance, then again, it is up to them to decide whether to stick around or leave. You're never going to want to change yourself, and you won't be able to do so. If you face such a person, in turn, then you really need to decide on whether to stay with that person or leave, because otherwise you'll be messing up your life and that of the other individual. That's a tough fact, but it's true. Narcissists are narcissists no matter whether they're with their family, at work or in a shop.

Can we really see ourselves from the sidelines? Can we at least understand, sense and feel us? It is hard to believe that we can, because if we could do that, we wouldn't have the frustrations and experiences of pain and unpleasant emotions. Even when we find, review and observe incompatibility in visual terms, we do not purposefully try to change it. Refined evil if very durable, it turns out, and without "surgical intervention" it won't go anywhere. Who feels greater psychological discomfort – the narcissist or the narcissist's partner? The partner has greater room for manoeuvre than the narcissist, because he can purposefully decide to "service" the narcissist or walk out the door. Narcissists, for their part, find it nearly impossible to understand that they are wrong, that they have made mistakes, that they are not ideal. Such people always feel that they must be perfect. As soon as they start to realise that they might be less than idea, they become aggressive and intolerable; the point is that they must defend their ideal nature. Often they attack or run away. And what happens to others who are involved? If a high threshold of mutual trust has been established (something that is hard for narcissists to do), then there is a chance for the narcissist to change, because in that case there is an understanding of how valuable the lost relationship really is. Narcissists cannot be close to just anyone. Others may scare them, and that is no bad thing. It's lonely to stay alone with your self-satisfaction if you have had at least one successful relationship with someone else in the past. Partners can make use of this fact if they want to continue relations with narcissists. Please be warned, however, that this is never going to be simple. Aristotle said long, long ago that it is stupid to tolerate the worst of the worst patiently if you do not have a sensible reason to do so.

What are the criteria that are used to evaluate individuals? Is it the question of whether communications, a life together or a working relationship can be established? Is the external appearance important? Is a narcissist always a precise, well-dressed and well-coiffed individual? No, that is more of a stereotype about a narcissist. Even those people who do not think much about their appearance fit in with one or another of the types of human beings. Whether they want to or not (and no one will ask whether they do or do not), they will be classified in accordance with a unifying system. Old maid, bachelor, careerist, gigolo, whore, homemaker, beauty specialist, blue-collar worker, intellectual, etc. People decide on these descriptions on the basis of clothing, style, speech, manners – and only then the content of what the individual has to say. We are prepared to listen to others and hear their texts only once we have satisfied our visual curiosity.

There is no point for anyone to worry about another person's appearance unless there is far-reaching personal interest. There's no need for you to share your aesthetic ideas unless the situation demands that you do so. If we want to "cure" someone, then we must set an example of tolerance, intellect and adequacy. Refined evil is an attempt to force your lifestyle on another in a relentless way and then to become offended if you fail. When the theme is initiated, you have to understand the goal if you are to reach that which is necessary. There are those who confirm themselves at the expense of others. They are afraid that what they have discovered is not of much use at all. If there is a personal belief, then there are no doubts about it, and no other evidence is needed. This is nothing new. Refined evil will try to ensure that the client, patient, child, neighbour, friend, husband or wife is similar to oneself. It would be odd if a psychoanalyst were to provide a patient with advice on style and fashion so that the patient could more easily find a sexual partner. And yet during individual discussions between client and psychotherapist, there is a whole series of processes which are not mentioned as such. An example is the aforementioned lack of teeth. The day comes when gestalt occurs, and the next time, the patient arrives with a set of gleaming teeth.

There can be different processes here. We can start with group therapy or individual therapy. Each method has its advantages in addressing problems. Speed and effectiveness. Results can be achieved in different ways, just as there are many ways to Rome – on foot, on the water, on land, by air...

Group therapy is not meant only to deal with visual goals, but it is one way to find yourself and gain materials for ongoing activities or analysis. In an individual consultation, the client digs up the information that is to be analysed from the field of information that has been identified in partnership with the psychotherapist. There are two sets of the subconscious in any session involving a client and a psychotherapist. The thing is that people are interested in the response that they create in others – how they look, greet others, speak to others, refuse things, admit things, inspire others or deny others. Individuals want to strengthen their own ideas about themselves, and this is something that can be achieved by being part of the community.

Clothes are objects, they are by no means emotions, but at the same time, they are a catalyst between individuals and the environments which they face. Clothes are a surface which limits the internal from the external. We always meet on this border at first, even in those cases when afterward we can no longer remember what the other person was wearing. When we gossip about others, visual appearance is often at issue: "Do you remember what she looked like at the party last night?!" Here we go back to jealousy. Envy about someone else's appearance and property. That's nothing new in this world.

How are prisoners all alike in visual terms? They all wear the same uniform. What points to social status externally? Clothing does. Clothing can help us differentiate between someone who is depressed and someone who is happy. A sick person will dress differently than a healthy person.

Yes, clothes are things, but they are imbued with emotions that we attach to them – that's true of everything that is around us. And what a spectrum of emotions there is here! An accessory becomes more important in the world of emotion if it expresses the spiritual and emotional richness of the person who presented it. If you lose a watch that you've worn for a long time, you may face not just a bad mood, but also emotional pain. It's even worse if the watch carried symbolic meaning – you bought it with your first salary, you got it from a lover. The watch itself may be nothing much, but you're going to remember the loss from time to time throughout your life. There have also been cases in your life, probably, when you run into someone and feel uncomfortable because you think you didn't look good, were not appropriately dressed, were not adequately prepared for the meeting, etc.

# WHY INDIVIDUALITY CONFRONTS WITH MASS?

Ever since there has been a social environment, people have been interested in at least two questions that have to do with visual appearance – ones that are asked by nearly everyone. Of course, this is not something that is seen as being in line with truly good manners, but people do manage to satisfy their correction. A classic example is this: If a woman is pregnant, people are first interested in who the father is. Second, they are interested in the woman's appearance now and previously, as well as in her clothing. People devote different amounts of energy in seeking out answers to these questions, but the foundation for these visual "questions" is that *Homo sapiens* has a base interest that is rooted in human nature. Why is this the case?

Our narcissistic side is what makes sure that we have this curiosity or yearning for knowledge. That is because a sexual partner or clothing is exactly that which we can see in order to form internal interpretations. The mechanism here is clear. It is not possible for people to change it, and there's really no reason to try to do so. If we all have such elements of narcissism, then we must seek to promote their productivity. What exactly do we want? Basically, none of us would have any complaints against anyone else if we were satisfied with our own outer appearance. In scientific terms, the narcissistic need would be satisfied.

Even in those ideal cases in which someone is completely satisfied with his or her outer appearance, however, the interest in another person's visual manifestations will not disappear. That is understandable, because that is I N F O R M A T I O N either about oneself through another or about another through oneself. This is information which allows us to learn, to improve ourselves, and to receive warning signals as to what we are dealing with at any specific moment in time. To be sure, visual appearances can be misleading. There are stereotypes which capture us. These are purposefully put to use by criminals. "She looked so elegant, but she turned out to be a crook" – how often have we heard something like that? External appearance relates to phenomenology in that it can lead to professional conclusions. There can be a certain appearance which suggests that the person is wealthy and, therefore, competent. There is a "click" of perception, and you choose that person above all others. Where does disappointment come into the picture? It appears when you end up being disappointed, because your stereotype turns out to be far from reality. The opposite can also be true – a person's appearance can be used to discover exactly that which is important and of value.

Refined evil strengthens against itself if you don't admit to your narcissistic needs. Do you know why? It is because you are perhaps afraid of them. There can be all kinds of reasons for this. You don't want to be too noticeable, perhaps, because that means responsibility. Or you may be afraid that you cannot provide for your own needs and interests. You can suspect that if you want something, you will not be able to stop in this regard, and your family will suffer. These, sadly, are fantasies about fear that are cultivated in society – the idea is that pursuing your narcissistic nature is bad and should be denounced. Why?

Because we interpret narcissism as an exaggeration – something that is excessive and may harm others. It is an ugly form of expression, because it might involve conceit, haughtiness and, most of all, selfishness. Refined evil is the upholding of this myth, because if we are not narcissists, we will lack the selfishness that ensures that we can do our work at as high a level of quality as possible.

Selfish individuals can collapse if they find out that the services that they have rendered have not been of a sufficient level of quality. People don't care about the results of their work only if their narcissism has been completely ignored. It doesn't matter what you do or how, the main thing is to get the salary. This means not a single iota of self-respect and self-admiration. There are lots of people who demonstrate such apathy. And yet you can ask any child whether his or her parents are beautiful, aromatic and handsome. Yes, the children will say. They have a narcissistic nature, and that means that they want their parents to be ideal.

If parents are overworked and are constantly banging on about money shortages, children cannot understand why they need so much clothing and other stuff if it is not used and is even denied. It may be that it is advantageous to interpret narcissism and egotism in such a direct and primitive way if we are not to spend the oh-so-desired money.

We are all informed of the fact that different political systems and strategic needs of businesses do not support individuality. Clients, subordinates and mutually dependent people are more convenient for businesses if they are obedient and, accordingly, frightened into submission. They are better than people who think independently, are stable, and are fully valuable individuals. In politics, in turn, what is most advantageous is a jealous society with a low level of self-confidence, because it is easier to manipulate those who are dependent. After all, not everyone can "tolerate" the fact that someone else looks good and, therefore, also feels good.

Parents manage to frighten their children in various ways and without even realising that they are doing so. Discrimination related to clothing is an example of this. A typical situation is one in which parents buy only the most elementary and necessary things, as well as those are cheapest – nothing more. Price dictates choice. Taste is of no importance. Saving money is the main thing!

So why would there be discrimination related to the child's clothing? It's because parents intuitively feel that this may prove to be more important than they want to admit. Stereotypes take the upper hand. If children get everything that they want, then the belief is that they will grow up as egotistical people. If they are too good looking, then they will marry too early. If they are unfamiliar with shortages, they will not be able to appreciate wealth, etc.

These ideas are not to blame in and of themselves, but they must be interpreted and perceived in a far less primitive way. Society has developed over the course of hundreds of thousands of years, and these positions remain important. For that reason, it's worth looking at the deeper thought that is hidden therein.

We know that eternal childhood hostility between brothers and sisters can be caused not by what one of them has, but by what they do not have. Small amounts of things must be divided up. Here, the importance issue is not the attention of parents, but the things themselves. Of course, that does not exclude parental attention. Parents are put into a situation in which there are few alternatives. Imagine a crumb of bread that has to be divided up for several hungry mouths. Children do not project this situation onto their parents, and they do not ask for another piece if they know that the parents don't have one. That's why children fight amongst themselves over those things which cannot be divided up in a friendly way.

# SELF-DISCOVERY THROUGH THE SURROUNDING VIEW

We also know that if people start sexual relations too early, that has to do less with how attractive they are, but instead with the attitude that others demonstrate. Young people want to feel valuable, appreciated, and a bit envied over achievements not just in education or sports, but also their appearance. Boys and girls want to be beautiful. If no one responds to them, they may try to attract attention by offering or accepting proposals of sex. A second common reason for starting a sexual life too early is the yearning for a father and mother if communication with parents is not sufficient. Teenagers can look for physical satisfaction which represents more in the way of psycho-emotional famine and loneliness. The concept "expensive" is a conditional one. It is better to buy something at the right time and place and then forget about the frustration that has begun. The possibility of an experience in the future can "cost" more. Insurance won't cover it, and you will have to pay for it from your own pocket or, in future, from that of your children. Why? It is because of complexes.

No one in the world wants to be ugly, and that applies to your children, too. Poverty is what provokes people into stealing, lying and avoiding responsibility – far more so than wealth does. If these are characteristics which take root in childhood, then the tendencies are preserved no matter how fine the financial indicators of the individual end up being. Those who did not have much benefits during their childhood may well end up greedy and impossible to satisfy without any reason even when they are much older.

It is possible that if I were to engage in a broader discussion about this observation, there would be opponents to say that not all families can buy expensive clothing for their children. What's more, I noted at the beginning of this chapter that the value of clothing is not as important as the extent to which it is appropriate for the relevant environment and situation. This, however, is an idea which each person is allowed to interpret and use as he or she will. Conflicts do not occur if there are no disputes. If children are to be healthy, smart and full of self-respect, then they must be trained to be that way. Parents often say with pride: "When I was a kid, that wasn't what happened, and I'm not a bad person at all." Parents can be quite snooty about being right, about their taste, and about the values of their age. This can affect the way in which children are raised. There are places in the big world where young people can develop themselves, where they can meet someone who is wiser, more beautiful and richer than their mother or father is. There is no reason to fear that children will discover this independently. On the contrary. Kids need to learn that there are lots of opportunities in the world. They don't have to feel that they are abandoning or betraying their parents. They must understand that this is simply evolution. It is easy to imagine the potential reaction of my opponents – it is not easy to change attitudes that have entered our everyday lives from different sources such as parents, spouses, acquaintances, a school, the place where one lives, or other external flows of information. This is a very serious set of attitudes, and it is hard to oppose it on an individual basis. It may seem that it is simpler and cheaper to go with the flow without thinking about, analysing or criticising anything. Refined evils love that – not spending or investing resources and then becoming offended over slight achievements. Jasmine tea is cheap and good. There's no doubt about that, but such certain claims do not exist about everything. It seems that there must always be investments, because we grow tired of things that are simple and good. That justifies progress. People got tired of walking around naked, and so they invented clothing and transportation. After a war, having just one skirt is very daring. In our narcissistic society today, however, it is a shortcoming.

People are social animals, and they are always affected by an interactive environment. They see and hear things. If we have only one set of clothes, then we become accustomed to the idea that that is all that we deserve. If others have something more, than we are different. The line has been cast, and people start to focus not on the joy or lesson of communications, but instead on their own value. The results of this can be different, because people have imagination. Thinking is like improvising a musical theme, but we must always remember that if we have unnecessary "suspicions" about ourselves, then we can pollute our own psyche. We can't find reasons for differences. If there is just intuition along with observations, that will make us even more frustrated.

There is no need to "prepare" ourselves, but our environment provokes us to do so. We've all read the Hans Christian Andersen story about the ugly duckling which turns into a beautiful swan – a bird which had tormented itself with doubt.

Each of us has his or her own perceptions, and that means that we each get sick differently. There are many different diseases, and there are equally many processes in being sick. People can try treatment which makes them better without realising it. Illnesses can be manifested as psychosis, with the body getting all messed up and losing any sense of reality. The pain is felt everywhere and nowhere. People can be sick for a short time or a long time irrespective of what the diagnosis is. Being sick is one of the most diverse ways of expressing oneself in this world – of course, if you assume that your body is you. You need time to become acquainted with your disease, but not just time. You can achieve quick results, but the psychotherapist will not always be convinced of them, because you cannot come to an understanding quickly of things that have been accumulated for years and years. Your psyche needs to assimilate your experience and restructure experiences. That cannot be done in a single psychotherapeutic session. For instance, no one can promise you eternal health. At the same time, however, we can have an influence on our experiences and our sufferings.

This is our individual responsibility in terms of ourselves and others. Psycho-hygiene is what is responsible for our mental and physical well-being. All kinds of fantasies and imagined concepts flow into these "variations." "My parents don't love me. They don't care about me. My parents are having a hard time in line, and I have to not only justify them as a child, but also understand them!" This last sentence may seem noble, but there are millions of other ways of training children to be empathetic. Why should this involve humiliation? Parents may be hypocrites if they claim that they have never been able to save up enough money to buy beautiful and appropriate clothing for their children. The word "price" is missing here, you see, and children receive different messages which they receive from your attitude. If you think that things that your children like are too expensive and you always say that "we don't have any money," then your conclusions are not true. This usually represents egocentrism on the part of the parents – an "inability" which they push onto their children's shoulders. Even during war parents have been able to delight their children with clothing. That, of course, means that the parents must be sufficiently adult in terms of understanding their position and their role. They must have empathy toward their children, and they must express their ego in an adequate way.

When children ask for too much clothing, that doesn't always have to do with a lack of attention or love on the part of their parents. As I noted, each case must be reviewed individually, and in any situation we can find solutions and explanations to problems. If you think that your children devote too much attention to their exterior, for instance, that may have to do with age crises and the internal conflicts of the children. Any preschool child who goes to a carnival wants to put on one of the costumes that he or she enjoys, because that means expression which involves identification with the abilities and the expressions of the selected hero.

The costume ensures this. Children can never be rabbits, because they cannot turn into animals, but if they put on a rabbit costume, they symbolise something nice, soft and fluffy. That is something of a projective test which allows children to tell their parents how they feel and what they wish to receive. If your children choose a Batman costume, then their psychological type is different than if they wore a rabbit costume. Of course, you have to ask your children why they want to dress up like film heroes, because Batman is not an unambiguous character. He represents a spark, enormous strength, courage and cleverness. There is no character who can do absolutely everything. It doesn't really matter which child chose a specific mask. What's important is to understand the difference among children, and you must not insist that they should change their costume or wear a different one that fits or has been received from older neighbours. I chose this example to offer a broader sense of psychological ideas about self-image. Nothing happens without motivation. Any internal encouragement leads us to do something with our exterior. When does a man unbutton the top button of his shirt? When does a woman put on a tight dress? There can be all kinds of reasons for this. It may be too hot. The collar may be too tight. The woman may have lost weight. Perhaps she has received a raise. The point is that we don't always have to perceive such actions in an excessively direct way.

Clothing has always been a reason for frustration in society. Childhood memories and the self-identification of adults lead each person to draw conclusions – like it, dislike it, it's good or bad, it's beautiful or ugly, it is necessary or unnecessary, etc. People need to think about clothing, but not everyone thinks about its true meaning. It is an object which must be touched and which must be seen every day throughout life. When people die, they are at least wrapped up in cloth. Burial firms today ask the deceased person's relatives about the colour palette which they prefer. Is that not odd? People should be allowed to make such judgments independently. Exterior appearance if of importance.

People project their emotions externally, presenting not just the characteristics that are typical of them themselves. People seek answers to their observations. There must be room between observations and answers in which information is collected. There can be several places where information can be found. In psychological terms, people look for places which are satisfactory to them. These "mines" are what quality of life is dependent on. They help to draw global conclusions about you and about others. Appropriateness is not always reality. Adaptation is a way of calming yourself down. It is a "bandage" for shortcomings, an excuse for a difficult childhood, an explanation as to why one cannot find a good place in society, an objection against youth or old age, or an argument in favour of laziness and jealousy. The way in which we think and the direction in which our thoughts go can end up in the "arms" of refined evil. When this closeness is felt, clothing no longer creates the illusion that all is well. Quite the opposite is true – you don't do as well as you would like. You can no longer fool yourself or others with your image, stories, promises and claims. If you review your reserves, then you can find that you can supplement them, seeking out those things that are lacking or those that you now need. Don't criticise yourself for the fact that your friends, interests, lifestyle, clothing or employment may change. Life is flexible – count on that. You can't spend a lot of time playing in a single sandbox. Summer comes to an end and you have to go back to school no matter if you want that to happen or not.

Those who remain in the "sandbox" usually engage in manipulations, because they lack knowledge about themselves. They don't know much about their abilities and opportunities. I know of a businessperson who used to dress himself and his wife in white designer clothes so as to leave the impression that he was an unforced free-thinker. The "necessary" people believed that this "white couple" would raise them into the heavens. A politician who is a good orator, has accepted a declaration prepared by others, and has learned it by heart can be elected to Parliament. A sassy woman who dresses up like an office worker offers advice to the parental committee at school. A police officer who catches someone in a traffic violation assigns a fine, does not prepare the paperwork, but treats the driver rudely. The manipulation proves to be successful in all of these cases. The images have been encouraged, because the addressees are foolish, and there is an insufficient set of intellectual and emotional information. Such clichés may be durable specifically because they are so simple. For instance, fear of psychological castration is not always a psychological problem. Instead, it can represent a lack of knowledge and a limitation in one's thinking.

We have arrived at the point of psychological thinking at which society's identity comes up against and confronts individual identity. It may be the case that few people can afford to wear clothing that is in line with their psychological essence, because they have problems within themselves and their environment. Eccentrics who behave in provocative ways that are far from the ideal tend to be rather different in terms of their mental health. The same is true of those who scrupulously observe unifying visual elements which turn them into clones. Perhaps the desire to exaggerate oneself or be similar to everyone else is what has promoted the economic crisis in the world. Expressive individualism and spirituality go lacking in this regard. It seems that this is a free niche in which people might find a place for themselves.

# UNFULFILLED LONGING
## OF THE LOOKS

Can a woman's purse mean something special? Freud wrote that this accessory symbolises the woman's vagina. When a woman respects her vagina, her pursue reflects projective self-respect. Women change this accessory in line with their clothing, the season, or their practical or aesthetic needs. We can conclude, therefore, that this self-understanding of women either shifts or is modified in the sense of its own self-improvement. This is not a concept that is to be perceived directly. It is an emotional expression when a woman puts on her clothes.

Men, too, have common gender characteristics which project the set of phallic elements. The car is the first thing. People whisper that a big car means one thing, and a little car means something else. Of course, the size of the car is of no importance at all. The model of a car which a man selects depends on his needs and his character. In this, the car is like a necktie, which is a more or less mandatory element in male apparel. The length of the tie says nothing, because if it did, what would we think about men who wear a butterfly tie? Temperament can be revealed by someone who is dressed in a potato sack, but only if that happens on purpose and not because of spiritual and, accordingly, material impoverishment. Anyone who is healthy and able to work can afford to buy a pair of trousers which fit, make sure that they're clean, and ascertain that they are pleasing to the eye and the body.

Excuses about this sometimes seem like something which envious people say. The idea that "you don't question someone else's taste" is presented by tasteless and inconsistent consumers. Here we are interested in the psychological aspects of the term. Fashion trends are dictated by the need to satisfy psychological needs. People today must take quick and dynamic decisions. We are psychologically prepared to receive tailor-made information or a specific informative picture in an advertisement. If the psyche is prepared for this model of perception, then this is a scheme which affects us in many different spheres.

A Russian fashion specialist called Y. Vasiliev has analysed fashion trends and found that clothes today are designed so that their wearers can always have sex very quickly. People are prepared for this, and they feel that this look is an advantage among other people. Other sources offer the thought that fashion is needed by the masses. If people don't know what to wear this season and how to style their hair, they will not be able to draw their own conclusions, and that may confuse them. Directions from the top are needed, and the greater the psychological unreadiness in society, the more panic and fear there will be. For instance, it is necessary to differentiate among and find new touchstones in a shifting environment, and so people need advice on how to think and prepare themselves for the next stage in life. Healthy people do not dither in psychological terms, they trust their own judgment first and foremost. They are psychologically mature people with adequate behaviour and image even in the most unimaginable situation. They are what they are. In their inner health and harmony, they make the most appropriate choices for themselves without humiliation or exaggeration. They are very good at arranging priorities, including external ones. They are happy and to be envied, because such people never lack anything.

Society yearns for beauty but is aggressive toward those who manage to be beautiful. Society wants a higher coefficient of wealth, but it is hostile toward those who achieve wealth. In different social areas, there is a bit of psychological pressure. Any place of employment has traditions which can be psychologically difficult to overcome. It is easier to adapt and to accept the infantile expressions of the environment. This can be something quite absurd, because people are unaware of what is happening. You turn up in a new dress, and everyone notices, but then you say that you bought this old thing accidentally, it was just a matter of circumstance. If someone compliments you, you feel that it is better to question the person's motivations than to say thank you. You tried on the clothes. You asked the saleslady to tell you how you looked. The saleslady doesn't know anything personal or special about you, so how is she supposed to recommend apparel to you? Of course, she may have empathy and a conscience, but the most that she will dare do is assess the size and the colour unless she has the special talent, interest and experience that allows her to step back from you. Otherwise there will be a reciprocal psychological link that will be in line with the saleslady, not you. Perhaps you're lucky enough to know what you are confirming with the purchase. The saleslady will always be a good mediator, and she will be very good at reflecting your subconscious in the conscious. I know of a young girl, a teenager, who travelled abroad, went to a store and discovered that she was no longer a child, she was an amazing young woman. There were dozens of dresses in the shop, but she was given a white and romantic dress that would be appropriate for an afternoon event. She was also given a black suit that was quite non-traditional in cut – a coat and knee pants. Everything fit, and the young woman could rise above her self-understanding as a teenager. She was delighted, and the sales personnel were delighted. A few months later, the girl told her mother that she could no longer wear her old clothing, because it made her feel childish and of lesser value. Shortly thereafter, and seemingly out of the blue, the young woman won a foreign language Olympiad, moved to a better school, and replaced absolutely all of her friends with new ones. She no longer smoked and drank, she came home in the evening, she didn't skip classes – she was a completely different woman. She had encountered a completely selfless woman who knew nothing personal about the girl, but encouraged her to go to the starting line of life because she precisely saw the girl's essence and materialised her imagination. The girl's mother no longer had the problem of harming her health by being disappointed in her daughter and by having to go to the police all the time. Instead, she knew that all that was necessary was to purchase two appropriate and fine pieces of clothing. We all know that things are there to serve people. The only issue is to choose those things correctly.

To reiterate, someone who looks good can cause feelings of jealousy – cause them, not create them. We create children, relationships art, etc., but feelings which gnaw at us from the inside as if they were syphilis are an evil psycho-emotional defect. Such feelings can be sensed not only in relation to strangers, but also among one's own – between parents and children, between married people. The foundation here can be a fear of competition. We don't want others to be more successful than ourselves in external terms. There are lots of fairy tales which speak to this – Snow White, Cinderella, the Snow Queen. These are fairy tales with another moral, too. If our external desires are unfulfilled, if we want to be more attractive, if we find is psychologically hard to survive the fear of castration because we are ugly and of lesser value, then euphoria about achievements in this area lead s to work hard in pursuit of victory. Fairy tale characters often find themselves in such difficulties. People need to understand this, because these characters are all based on true prototypes. When given a choice, children will always and automatically take the side of that which is beautiful and good, but some people lose that ability when they grow up. Those who do not feel a sense of sympathy because of their own personal difficulties do not necessarily die as wicked people. Some do, but others do everything possible to get to the point where they support that which is good and beautiful. That is a test in life. Those who fail the test don't want to lose, and they subconsciously choose to be like everyone else so as not to annoy others and to weaken their phobias about failure. This is no exaggeration. Even married people can, whether consciously or subconsciously, compete with one another in visual terms and feel envy and jealous. That is nothing new for humanity.

It is hard to conceive and believe in the idea that there is generational jealousy in which one of the parents tries to oppress the sexual identity of a child, whether of the same or the opposite gender. It is clothing which emphasises differences, age and mood. If parents do not tell children what suites them, do not tell them that clothing must be chosen in line with the proportions of the body, and do not move children toward a visually successful and promising image, then the risk is that each generation will have an increasing chance to repeat the same mistakes and fail to understand why this repetition is so evil. Of course, this can be interpreted and explained in various ways. Psychological effect is the unifying element in all cases. People who have power and influence make use of their advantages – parents in relation to children, spouses in relation to one another, friends, acquaintances and colleagues among themselves. Think of a family which has a son and a daughter who are close in age. The mother implements her parental feelings more toward the son than the daughter. She feels that he is more sensitive than the daughter. He was allowed to sleep in his parents' bed until he was 12, but that is not the point of the story. The mother exaggerated her desire to push the son forward while devaluing the role of the daughter in the family. The woman implemented her feminine identity through her son, because she could not do the same with her husband. The son was the "good and nice person" before which the mother could preen, and the daughter was a competitor without anyone in the story really realising this. Thus the mother took revenge for her experiences in the past. Later the daughter would complain that she could not remember a single instance in which her mother praised her for her appearance. On those instances when the mother showed and interest, it was via a denying and negative attitude. The daughter also felt that her brother was good looking. Their mother carefully chose his clothes and made sure that she devoted enough time and money to him. She chose her daughter's clothing carelessly and even with a bit of intolerance. The young woman remembers one such instance very vividly: She and her mother were trying on identical white blouses. They both looked into the mirror. The blouses were the same, but the appearance differed. The mother immediately saw that her daughter looked much better in the same blouse, and she tried to point the girl toward a different piece of clothing. This can be attributed to nothing other than jealousy and envy. The young woman didn't change her elementary school hairdo until she was in her 30s. She wore a ponytail and no makeup at all. That wasn't because she didn't want to change things, she was just afraid. Her mother didn't recommend that she emphasise the various elements of her face. Her lips were not distinct, the mother recommended transparent lip gloss. He eyelids were too big for eye shadow, her eyebrows came together into a single line and caused her to appear angry, her neck was too long to wear necklaces, her skirts had to be long enough to cover her ugly needs. Her earlobes were too long, and earrings would simply accent the "frightening" disproportion. All of this was something which the daughter "learned" from her mother. There were few positive statements, but there were lots and lots of complaints about the girl's appearance. What exactly is violence in the family? Does it have to be physical in nature? Psychological violence is hard to prove, as is the fact that parents take out their complexes by demonstrating their power over their children. Manipulation with clothing is a fairly common thing.

In concluding this chapter, I would like to add that there are many, many material things in this world that have been created by people – wonderful, wise, aware and talented people. The creator of each thing has an audience of consumers. There is always a conflict between the good and the bad. We wear our own psychological "content." The peel of a carrot tells us about the soil in which it grew. We can hope for something different, but it will never be the case that if we envy and scorn others, we will become the best of the best. We can feel momentarily better at the expense of others, but we will not become happier, because it is always and inevitably a short-term thing.

No generation has made do without clothing. We can consciously evaluate what clothing tells each of us. We can know what it provides to us in psycho-emotional terms. It may be that this process of self-discovery will allow us to find something even more valuable. That depends on you and your personal life story. In that case, you can justify the hope that clothing can provide a good mood, as well as achievements in love and health.